Contents

Any words appearing in the text in bold, **like this**, are explained in the Glossary.

Can I see all the stars in the sky?

On a moonless night, far away from the bright lights of houses and city streets, you can see about 2,000 sparkling stars. The tiny specks of light you see at night are from stars that are thousands of billions of kilometres away. Each of these stars has its own special life story.

Our Sun is just an ordinary star like many of the others in the sky. It looks much bigger and brighter because it is a lot closer to us than the other stars. There are many distant stars in space that are much larger and more powerful than the Sun.

Thousands of stars can be seen on a dark, moonless night. The band from top to bottom in this picture is called the Milky Way.

THE UNIVERSE

Stars and Constellations

Revised and Updated

Dr Raman K. Prinja

www.heinemann.co.uk/library
Visit our website to find out more information about Heinemann Library books.

To order:
☎ Phone 44 (0) 1865 888066
▤ Send a fax to 44 (0) 1865 314091
💻 Visit the Heinemann Bookshop at www.heinemann.co.uk/library to browse our catalogue and order online.

First published in Great Britain by Heinemann, Halley Court, Jordan Hill, Oxford, OX2 8EJ, part of Pearson Education.
Heinemann is a registered trademark of Pearson Education Ltd.

Editorial: Nick Hunter and Rachel Howells
Design: Richard Parker and Manhattan Design
Illustrations: Art Construction
Picture Research: Mica Brancic
Production: Julie Carter

Originated by Modern Age
Printed in China by Leo Paper Group

ISBN 9780431154756 (hardback)
11 10 09 08 07
10 9 8 7 6 5 4 3 2 1

ISBN 9780431154886 (paperback)
12 11 10 09 08
10 9 8 7 6 5 4 3 2 1

British Library Cataloguing in Publication Data
Prinja, Raman, 1961-
Stars and constellations. - 2nd ed. - (The universe)
1. Stars - Juvenile literature 2. Constellations - Juvenile literature
I. Title
523.8
A full catalogue record for this book is available from the British Library.

Acknowledgements
The Publishers would like to thank the following for permission to reproduce photographs: Bridgeman Art Library (National Library of Australia) p. 13; Corbis p. 11 (bottom); NASA pp. 5, 18, 21, 27, 29; Science Photo Library pp. 4, 6, 7, 11 (top), 14, 16, 17, 19, 20, 23, 24, 25, 26, 28.

Cover photograph reproduced with permission of Science Photo Library/Jason Ware.

The publishers would like to thank Geza Gyuk of the Adler Planetarium, Chicago, for his assistance in the preparation of this book.

Every effort has been made to contact copyright holders of any material reproduced in this book. Any omissions will be rectified in subsequent printings if notice is given to the publishers.

The stars in our skies are only some of the 100 billion stars that make up our **galaxy**. All the rest are too faint and far away to be seen with just our eyes. A galaxy is a huge collection of stars, held together by the force of **gravity**. There are perhaps 100 billion galaxies in the **universe**.

The galaxy that is home to our **solar system** (and to all the stars we see in the sky), is called the Milky Way. It gets its name from a misty white band of millions of stars that stretches across the sky.

This is a picture of the Whirlpool Galaxy, which looks a little like our Milky Way Galaxy. Galaxies are made of billions of stars.

The milky band that makes up the Milky Way can really only be seen in dark skies well away from city lights. The stars in our **galaxy** give us some of the most amazing sights in space.

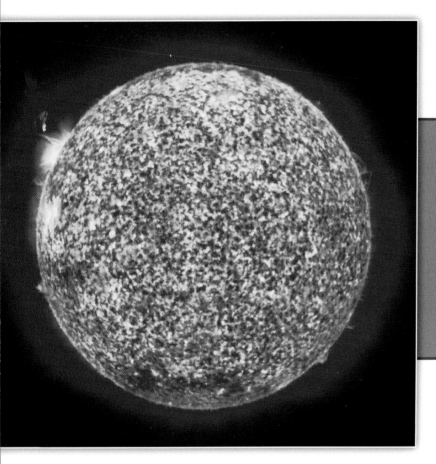

All the stars, like the Sun, are huge balls mostly made of boiling hot **hydrogen** gas. The stars have no solid surface. They are very different from rocky planets like Earth.

What are "wandering stars"?

Thousands of years ago people spotted that five "stars" in the sky moved much faster than all the others. The ancient Greeks worshipped them as five gods. Today we know that these "wandering stars" are not really stars, but the planets Mercury, Venus, Mars, Jupiter and Saturn.

Stars don't really move during the night!

If you go out after dark and choose a bright star, then come back and look for it a few hours later, you will find that it is no longer where you first saw it! It will now be towards your west. Just as the Sun and Moon rise in the east and set in the west, so do the stars.

The stars aren't really travelling east to west every night. They seem to move because the Earth on which you are standing is spinning on its **axis**.

As the Earth spins on its axis, the stars seem to move around us. To create this image of the stars "moving" across the sky, the camera's shutter was kept open for 6 hours as the Earth turned.

What are constellations?

Thousands of years ago our ancestors began to recognize patterns, or groups of stars in the sky at night. Year after year they could see the patterns rising and setting. These patterns of stars are called **constellations**.

Constellations are not real. They are totally imaginary ways of grouping stars that poets, farmers and **astronomers** have made up over the past 6,000 years.

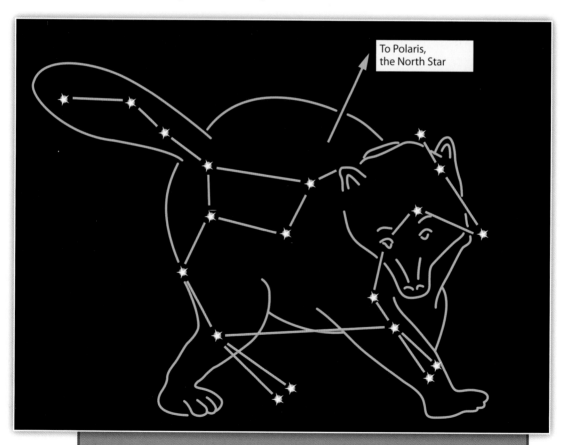

To Polaris, the North Star

This diagram shows the constellation of Ursa Major, or the Great Bear – often seen in the sky during spring (see page 10).

Connecting the dots

As time passed, the ancient people began to form the shapes of animals or creatures out of the star patterns. They were imagining lines drawn between a few stars to make shapes from stories in their **myths**. They were playing "join the dots" with the stars. For example, the constellation of Draco is named after the picture of a dragon that is traced out after connecting lines between at least fifteen different stars.

A few common constellations

The constellations were first made up a long time ago. Today, in cities with bright street lights, it can be hard to make them out. Also, most of the constellations don't really look much like the people or animals after which they were named! So don't worry if you can't find the bull in Taurus, or the lion in Leo.

Earth's **equator** is an imaginary line that divides the planet into two halves, the northern **hemisphere** and the southern hemisphere. You will see a different set of constellations depending on which side of the equator you live.

Eighty-eight constellations

Today our entire sky is divided into 88 constellations. They join up to cover the whole sky, just as countries fill the map of a continent on Earth. Different cultures around the world have different amounts and names of constellations. Thousands of years ago Chinese astronomers divided the sky into just 28 constellations.

In the northern hemisphere

Here are four **constellations** you can look out for if you live in the northern **hemisphere**.

In spring: Try to find the constellation called Ursa Major or the Great Bear (shown on page 8). During spring it is high above the northeast horizon. Inside the pattern of the Great Bear is a smaller one made of seven stars called the Plough (or Big Dipper).

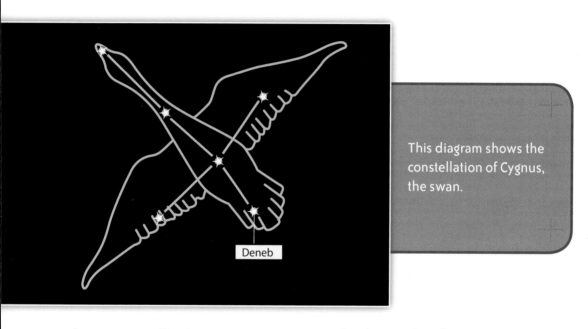

Deneb

This diagram shows the constellation of Cygnus, the swan.

In summer: During summer you can look out for the constellation called Cygnus, which is the **Latin** name for swan. It rises high in the sky during the evenings. The brightest star in Cygnus is called Deneb, which marks the tail of the swan.

In autumn: An easy constellation to spot in autumn is Cassiopeia. In Greek **myths** a queen called Cassiopeia was placed among the stars by the sea-god Poseidon. Cassiopeia looks like a wide letter "W", made of five bright stars. It is best seen high in north-eastern skies during November.

In winter: A beautiful constellation seen in winter is Orion. It is named after a great hunter in ancient Greek myths. Orion has the shape of a large rectangle, but it is meant to show the shape of the hunter! Three bright stars in a row make up the hunter's belt that holds a sword. Two bright stars called Betelgeuse and Rigel mark the left shoulder and the right foot of the hunter.

In the southern hemisphere

People living in the southern hemisphere can see 32 constellations in the skies. Many of these were named only a few hundred years ago when scientists and explorers went from the north to the south of the **equator** for the first time.

The most famous of these constellations is called Crux, or the Southern Cross. It even appears on the national flags of Australia and New Zealand.

Betelgeuse

Rigel

This is the constellation of Orion, the hunter.

The national flag of Australia shows the constellation of the Southern Cross.

How do people use constellations?

Constellations can be very useful for finding stars. On a dark, cloudless night you can see thousands of stars with your eyes (and millions more with a **telescope**). Trying to tell which star is which can be very difficult. The constellations help us to pick out the bright stars by breaking up the sky into parts. This is just like the way it is easier to find towns and cities on a map when a country is divided into counties or states.

This beautiful indigo bunting bird was photographed in Texas, USA.

Birds use the stars too!

During a year some birds can migrate thousands of kilometres from one part of the globe to another. How do the birds find their way? While some use features like rivers, coasts and mountains, other birds watch the stars to find their way! On clear nights, birds such as the indigo bunting can travel by watching patterns of stars in the sky, in just the same way that sailors used the constellations.

For hundreds of years, **astronomers** used the positions of the stars and constellations to find out the exact time. They used special telescopes that could not be moved from side to side. Every time Earth completes one turn on its **axis**, the same stars appear in front of the telescope. Astronomers can read the stars to tell the time, just as we would read the numbers on a clock.

Sailors used to rely on the stars to work out where they were and the direction they needed to sail in.

How did ancient people use constellations?

Ancient people used the constellations to tell the time of year. They noticed where groups of stars were at different times of the year. Since different constellations can be seen during the year, they can be used to tell what month it is. This was a big help to farmers. Using the constellations, they knew it was time to plant the crops or harvest them.

What is a star made of?

People have always wondered what the stars are, and how they were made. It is only in the past 100 years or so that scientists have begun to understand what the stars are made of, how they work and how they change. Scientists now know that stars are giant balls of incredibly hot gas. They are mostly made of **hydrogen** gas and don't have any solid surfaces. Stars have different regions or layers. The outer layers are the only ones that we can see directly, and they have temperatures of about 3,000 to 30,000°Celsius.

The hydrogen gas in the centre, or core, of a star is even hotter. It is being squeezed and as this happens it gets hotter. It reaches temperatures of many millions of degrees Celsius. The energy that is made in this boiling hot core is what makes the stars and our Sun shine.

This picture shows the **supergiant** star called Betelgeuse, which is part of the **constellation** of Orion.

Hot stars, cool stars

There are two things that you can easily notice about stars in the night sky. Firstly, they are not all the same colour. Some stars are blueish, some are yellow-white, and others are reddish. The stars have different colours because they have different temperatures. The Sun is a medium-hot, yellow-white star. The blueish stars are much hotter than the Sun, and the red stars are cooler. Blue stars are usually younger than the red stars.

The second thing to notice is that some stars are brighter than others. Stars can appear brighter in the sky either because they are more powerful or because they are much nearer to us (like the Sun). In just the same way, the light from a torch can seem bright either because the battery inside is strong, or because the torch is held near to you.

How big are the stars?

Our **galaxy** has 100 billion stars of many different sizes. Although the Sun is almost 1.4 million kilometres (865,000 miles) across, it is just a medium sized star! There are giant stars in space that can be 100 times larger than the Sun. There are also dwarf stars that can be 100 times smaller.

Arcturus

Sun

Aldebaran

This diagram shows the size of the Sun in comparison with Arcturus, which is a **red giant** star, and Aldebaran, which is a supergiant star.

How far away are the stars?

The Sun is 150 million kilometres (93 million miles) away from us. Most of the other stars are millions of times further away. Light travels faster that anything we know. It moves at 300,000 kilometres (186,000 miles) per second, but still takes 8 minutes to reach us from the Sun.

Light takes around four years to reach us from the next nearest star. Remember there are at least 100 billion other stars in the Milky Way. It would take almost 100,000 years for light to reach us from the furthest stars in the Milky Way. The light shining from billions of stars in a neighbouring **galaxy** to ours, called the Andromeda Galaxy, takes 2 million years to reach us!

This dazzling mixture of different stars was seen using the Hubble Space **Telescope**. The stars have different colours, depending on their temperatures. Most blue stars are young and hot, while red stars are older and cooler.

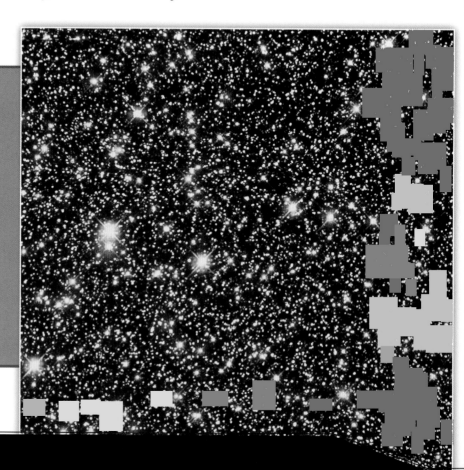

The Milky Way and Andromeda are just two of the more than 100 billion galaxies that make up the **universe**. It would take over 10 billion years for light to reach us from stars in the most distant galaxies that we can see.

This spiral galaxy is very similar in size and shape to our own galaxy, the Milky Way, but is 15 million **light years** away from Earth!

A scale model

Imagine Earth scaled down to the size of the full stop at the end of this sentence. On this scale, the Sun would be about the size of a golf ball, placed about 3 metres (10 feet) away. The next nearest star would be 540 miles (870 kilometres) away in our model. The entire Milky Way would be a giant plate that is 20 million kilometres (12 million miles) across, which is almost half the distance to the **orbit** of Venus!

How are stars made?

One star like the Sun is born somewhere in our **galaxy** every year. Stars are made out of huge clouds of **hydrogen** gas and dust. These giant clouds are called **nebulae.** *Nebula* is the **Latin** name for mist.

The nebulae can be a million times bigger than the distance between the Sun and the furthest planet in our **solar system**, Neptune. This distance is about 4,500 million kilometres (2,800 million miles). Each nebula can hold enough gas and dust to make thousands of stars. The **constellation** of Orion has a star-making nebula in it.

Squashed by gravity

The gas in a nebula is slowly squashed together by the force of **gravity**, a little like the way you might gather loose snow to make a hard snowball. After a few million years a lot of gas in space is brought together into a tightly squashed ball. This giant ball becomes hotter and hotter.

New stars are being made in these huge pillars of gas and dust called the Eagle Nebula.

When a star is born

Slowly the temperature at the centre of the ball of gas reaches an incredible 15 million°Celsius. Something special then happens to this very hot, and tightly packed gas. The hydrogen is changed into a different gas called helium. This is called a **nuclear fusion reaction**.

Whenever nuclear fusion happens in the ball of hot gas, a lot of energy is released. This is the energy that makes a star shine brilliantly. When nuclear reactions start, a star is born!

This is an artist's idea of a Jupiter-like planet orbiting another star like our Sun.

Where do planets come from?

Some gas and dust is usually left over after the star has been made. Over millions of years, this extra material is gathered into small clumps by the force of gravity. The clumps then crash into each other and grow larger. Finally these clumps of rocky material become planets that **orbit** the newly born star. Scientists think that there may be many millions of stars with their own planets in our galaxy.

How long do stars shine?

The stars in the sky are not all the same. Some of them are young, many are middle-aged, and a few are very old. Stars don't live forever. After they are born, they change over billions of years and then they die. A bright star that you can see shining in a **constellation** today might not be there billions of years from now.

Life stories

When a star is first made in a **nebula**, it can be a massive heavyweight star or a small lightweight one. The life stories of these two types of stars are different.

Lightweight stars like the Sun

The Sun is a lightweight star, born about 5 billion years ago. It shines constantly by using the fuel from hot **hydrogen** gas in the **nuclear fusion reactions**. In about 5 billion years from now this fuel supply will run out!

This group of stars are in the constellation of Gemini.

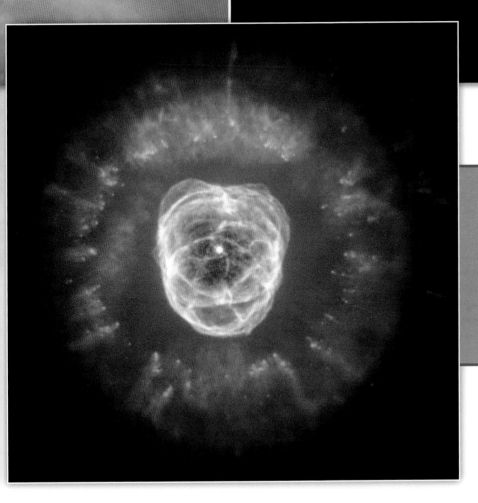

This is a planetary nebula called the Eskimo. The dying star began throwing out material about 10,000 years ago.

When any star runs out of fuel, big changes take place. In around 5 billion years, the Sun will swell up and become a huge, but cooler, star. Because its temperature will be lower, it will have a reddish colour. These types of stars are called **red giants**. When the Sun is a red giant it will swallow the planets Mercury and Venus, and perhaps even Earth. At the very least, Earth's **atmosphere** will be scorched and the oceans will boil away. All life on Earth will come to an end.

After they become red giants, light stars puff away a lot of their gas. The layers blown away by the star make an object called a **planetary nebula**. It is made of hot gas that was once part of the outer regions of the star. There are many beautiful and colourful planetary nebulae in our **galaxy** today. A planetary nebula is a sign that a star is dying.

All that is left behind of the lightweight star is its small core or central part. The core will be crushed by **gravity** into a tiny star about the size of Earth. This is called a **white dwarf**. A white dwarf star is made of very tightly packed **carbon** material. More than 5 billion years from now, the Sun will end its life as a white dwarf. The white dwarf star starts off at nearly 100,000°Celsius, and cools over billions of years, to become just a cold and dark object in space.

This diagram shows the size of a white dwarf star in comparison with the Sun and the Earth. The life of the Sun will end as a white dwarf star.

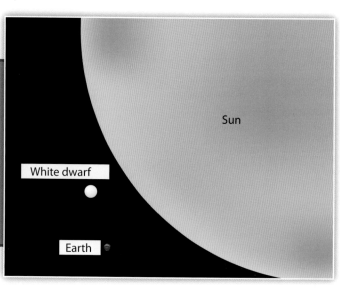

Sun

White dwarf

Earth

Stars much heavier than the Sun

There are massive stars in space that are between 10 to 100 times heavier than the Sun. The lives of these stars are much shorter than that of the Sun. This is because they are very powerful stars, and they burn their supply of **hydrogen** fuel very quickly.

When it is only about 10 million years old, a massive star can already be heading towards an explosive death. Its outer layers swell up hugely. The star becomes a **supergiant** that may be hundreds of times larger than the Sun is today. Two stars called Betelgeuse and Rigel in the **constellation** of Orion are supergiant stars.

Out with a bang

The supergiant star will end its life with a huge explosion called a **supernova**. When the star's supply of fuel for **nuclear fusion reactions** has run out, the supernova will blast the star apart in just a few seconds! This is one of the most powerful explosions known in the **universe**. The huge star is almost totally destroyed.

Anything left behind after this amazing supernova will be squeezed and crushed by the force of gravity. The once huge star may end up as either a **neutron star** or a **black hole**. We take a look at both of these incredible objects in the next chapter.

Massive stars will shatter in violent supernova explosions like the one shown in this computer drawing.

How will the stars end their lives?

Lightweight stars like the Sun end their lives as **white dwarf** stars. Much heavier stars end their lives as **neutron stars** or **black holes**. These are three of the strangest and most mysterious objects in space.

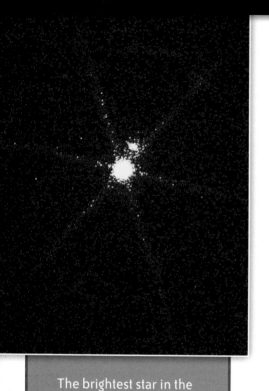

The brightest star in the night sky is called Sirius. The tiny star next to it is a white dwarf star.

Earth-sized white dwarf

A white dwarf star is usually only slightly larger than Earth, yet it weighs about half as much as the Sun. This means that the gas in the star is squeezed very tightly together. If you could bring a spoonful of white dwarf material to Earth, it would weigh as much as a tractor!

More than half of the 100 billion stars in our **galaxy** will end up as white dwarf stars. Because they are so small, **astronomers** have to use powerful **telescopes** to find them.

Neutron stars

A neutron star is formed after a star that weighs up to 20 times more than the Sun, explodes as a **supernova**. A neutron star is even stranger than a white dwarf. All the **matter** in this tiny star has been squeezed by **gravity** into a ball the size of a city, perhaps only 10 kilometres (6.25 miles) across. A spoonful of its material would weigh as much as a large mountain on Earth.

Black holes – no way out!

A black hole forms after a star that weighs more than 20 times the weight of the Sun, blows up in a supernova explosion. Black holes are the most mysterious objects in space. Gravity squeezes the leftovers of the dying star into an incredibly tiny space. If you could take the Earth and crush it into the size of a grape, you would end up with a black hole!

A black hole is a region of space in which the pull of gravity is so strong that nothing can ever escape from it. Even light, which is the fastest thing in the **universe**, cannot get out. So they don't shine at all and that's why they are called black holes.

An artist's idea of swirling hot gas and dust being sucked into a black hole.

How do we study stars?

Scientists who study the stars are called **astronomers**. To learn more about what the stars are made of and how they change, the astronomers use giant **telescopes**. The telescopes let them see very faint objects in great detail.

The bigger and higher, the better

The largest optical telescopes in the world are almost 10 metres across. They are usually placed on very high mountains, far away from bright city lights.

Even at these great heights, the Earth's **atmosphere** can ruin the view of the stars. The air is always shaking and moving and this is what makes the stars twinkle at night. This movement makes the stars look blurry through telescopes on the ground.

It is far better if the telescope is placed above Earth's atmosphere – in space. This is exactly what was done for one special telescope.

These giant telescopes, called Keck I and II, have been built on a mountain 4,200 metres high in Hawaii.

The Hubble Space Telescope

On 24 April 1990, the Hubble Space Telescope was launched into space on a **Space Shuttle** rocket. The telescope is in **orbit** 600 kilometres (370 miles) above Earth. It is controlled using radio signals sent from Earth. Astronauts have been back, since 1990, to visit the telescope, to fit new parts and carry out repairs.

The Hubble Space Telescope is very powerful and allows scientists to see objects that are deep in space, clearly. Many of the pictures in this book were taken using this telescope.

This is a view of the Hubble Space Telescope floating in orbit around the Earth.

The first telescopes

- Galileo Galilei was the first person to use a telescope for astronomy. In 1611 he used it to discover that the Sun had **dark spots**.
- In 1672 Sir Isaac Newton made the first telescope to use mirrors instead of lenses. This idea was very important.
- Scientists then learnt that the width of the mirror in a telescope was more important than the telescope's length.
- In 1673 Johannes Hevelius built a telescope that was 42.5 metres long. It was hard to use, as even the slightest wind would make it flutter.
- By 1948 a 5 metre wide telescope was built on Palomar Mountain in California.
- Today, some of the best telescopes in the world are on the island of Mauna Kea in Hawaii and on mountain ranges in Chile in South America.

Fact File

Here are some interesting facts about stars:

Galaxy of stars – Our Milky Way Galaxy is made of 100 billion stars. There are many different types of stars in our galaxy.

Nearest – The nearest star to Earth after the Sun is called Proxima Centauri. It is still 270,000 times further away from us than the Sun. If you imagine travelling in a spaceship at a speed of 50,000 kilometres per hour (30,000 miles per hour), it would take almost 90,000 years to reach Proxima Centauri!

Brightest – The brightest star in the sky after the Sun is called Sirius. It is in the **constellation** of Canis Major.

Most powerful – One of the most powerful stars known is called the Pistol star. It shines with 10 million times more power than the Sun.

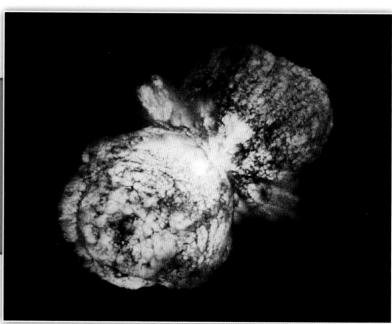

In the centre of this cloud of gas and dust is the doomed star Eta Carina. One day soon it will explode as a **supernova**.

The **universe** has 100 billion galaxies, and each galaxy has billions of stars.

Largest – The largest known star is a **supergiant** star called mu Cephei. It is around 3,700 times bigger than the Sun. If mu Cephei were placed at the centre of our **solar system**, it would probably swallow all the planets up to Saturn, and almost reach the planet Uranus.

Hottest – The hottest known star is a **white dwarf** star at the centre of a **planetary nebula** called NGC2440. This tiny star's outer layers have a temperature of 200,000°Celsius, which is 30 times hotter than the Sun.

Numbers
One thousand is written as 1,000. One million is 1,000,000 and one billion is 1,000,000,000.

Glossary

astronomer scientist who studies objects in space, such as planets and stars

atmosphere layers of gases that surround a planet

axis imaginary line around which a planet or moon spins

black hole invisible object in space that forms when a very massive star is crushed by gravity

carbon element in all living things

constellation imaginary pattern or picture formed in the sky by a group of stars

dark spot cooler patch sometimes seen on the Sun. It is also known as a sunspot.

equator imaginary line around the middle of Earth

galaxy collection of millions or billions of stars, gas and dust. We live in a galaxy called the Milky Way.

gravity force that pulls all objects towards the surface of Earth, or any other planet, moon or star

hemisphere half of the Earth between the North or South Pole and the equator

hydrogen colourless, odourless gas, which is easily set on fire

Latin language of the ancient Romans

light year distance that light travels in one year (nearly 6 million, million miles)

matter substance that all things are made of

myth old story told to explain how something came to be

nebula cloud of gas and dust in space. New stars are made in some nebulae.

neutron star highly squashed remains of a dead star, which spins very quickly

nuclear fusion reaction process where light substances are joined to make heavier ones, releasing enormous amounts of energy

orbit path taken by an object as it moves around another body (planet or star). The Moon follows an orbit around the Earth.

planetary nebula cloud of gas seen surrounding stars like the Sun when they run out of energy and begin to die

red giant cool star that has swollen to a much larger size than the Sun is today

solar system group of eight planets and other objects orbiting the Sun

Space Shuttle vehicle used by people to travel into space and orbit Earth

supergiant very swollen star that may be thousands of times larger than the Sun

supernova very bright and violent explosion of a huge star

telescope instrument used by astronomers to study objects in outer space

universe whole of space and its contents of matter and energy, including all planets, galaxies and stars

white dwarf very hot, small object formed when stars like the Sun run out of energy and die

More books to read

Stars and Planets: 10, Jacqueline Milton
(Oxford University Press, 2003)
Stars and Planets, Carole Stott (Kingfisher Books, 2005)
The Sun and Other Stars, John Farndon (Franklin Watts, 2003)

Index